CW00447892

1

It is within you

by

Soul Charmer

S. C. D. O.

It is within you

Dedicated to:

Me, You, US

about

It is
within
You

A puzzle is made of small
pieces that go together in a
specific order

We are just like a puzzle,
where our experiences are our
pieces that get entangled
during our life, building who
we really are.

This book is an exaltation of
oneself.

It's a book about me, you, us
and our singularity!!

It is

within you

The hardest choice
of your whole life
will be to finally
accept who you really are
and what you really want
and ultimately,
be in peace with all of it!

Allow yourself to see the
imperfections
Allow yourself to feel the pain
Allow yourself to be sad
Allow yourself to get hurt
Allow yourself to cry
Allow yourself to suffer
Allow yourself to bleed
Allow yourself to feel!

You will value yourself more
If you allow yourself to be **Yourself**
If you allow yourself to go through
the walks of hell that were destined
to you to walk through
If you allow yourself to taste the
bitterness
of your own being,
the being living in your deepest
core
If you allow yourself to rejoice
in your own Toxicity

You will value yourself more
if you allow yourself to be yourself

Just allow yourself
And thrive in Yourself

The hard part is to let go...

Let go of pain
Let go of relationships
Let go of anger
Let go of frustration

The hard part is to let go...

Let go of an idea
Let go of a dream
Let go of a routine
Let go of a memory

But the hardest of it all
Is to let go of, "Me"!

You allowing yourself to be…
That's the hardest "let go" of it all…

The "allow yourself to be"
while letting go, of who you thought you
were

All you are is in your brain!

Not in your mirror
or in a picture frame...
Not in someone else's words
or your Instagram posts...

All you are is in your brain!

Live your life
In a way
You feel like
You are always peaking!

It is within You

Everyone is desperate
to believe in something,
to believe in someone…
Why is that
no one believes in themselves?

Everyone follows the crowd
Everyone searches the most
empty personality
Just to bow down…
To do what they do,
dress how they dress,
think their thoughts
repeat their vain words…
Why is that
no one believes in themselves?

Everyone's fighting for equality
Hypocrites!
You're already all the same,
following the trends,
Blindly
What they do
is what you have to do…
Why is that
No one believes in themselves?

[It's within you, to believe in yourself]

The ones telling you
to be yourself,
are normally the first ones
judging you for not being
Like themselves...

It is within You

Never wait on anyone
to tell you that you are ready!

If you are,
You won't need them to tell you that,
You'll show them that!

[own it]

Build "Yourself"

Life will change,
Friends will go,
People will talk
People will make judgmental and
depreciative
comments in your name...
Some won't understand you
Some will ridicule you
Some will even leave you...

Fuck them all!!!
Build Yourself...

Let your work talk for you
Let them talk shit
Let them leave
and later crawl back
Let them Judge
and then regret
Let them make fun
and then ask for some!

Fuck it all!!!

Build **Yourself**!

Always be ready to set
the Ocean on fire!

The idea is not to convince the others
as one gets convinced by observation

The goal is to convince Yourself
and the rest will manifest!

[You can do it!]

In your life,
everyone can give
up on you,

but You!

Just because they hate on you,
You don't have to hate on
Yourself too!

If you see yourself in one way,
and the whole world sees you in a
completely different way,
Who would you believe in?

[Yourself, always Yourself...]

Most of the times,
the frustration arises
from the simple fact
that you are competing
only against your inner self,
and still manage to
end up in second place…

[don't let the social voice win! You can do this!]

It is within You

What if there was no fear?
Would you do whatever?
Not looking in the rearview mirror?

What if there was no fear?
Would you risk it all?
Being not afraid of the fall?

What if there was no fear?
Would you close your eyes
and jump?
Not afraid of the bump?

What if there was no fear?
Would you change your life?
Let go of all the strife?

What if there was no fear?
Would your choices be different?
Would you stop,
being your own life's figurant?

But...
What if all there is, is fear?
Will you reach your full potential?
Will you at least be near?

What if all there is, is fear?
Will you run from yourself?
Will you not ask for help?

Either way,
It is up to you…
Pave your own path
And stay
True to yourself

Whatever you are doing
Do it for You!!!

Mantra

I don't create expectations
I don't wish for material stuff
I don't dream about being someone else

I am happy for being able to experience
life as it is presented to me
I am happy for what I temporarily own
I am happy about Myself!

For all you loners
All of you that suffer in silence
All of you hiding behind the fence
All of you looking away in fear
All of you with no one near

I care!!!

For all you loners
All of you living in the dark
All of you that lost the spark
All of you socially awkward
All of you that have been cornered

I care!!!

For all you loners
You are not alone!

You're bigger than anything!
It is within you

We are all a Caran d'Ache pencil box
Some black, red, green, purple or yellow
But, only a few of us live life in the
rainbow

[The choice is within you]

It is within You

Just because everyone is running
You do not have to run too
Be patient and walk if needed
Your goals are yours to achieve

Just because everyone is settled
You do not have to settle too
Be patient and do not rush it
Your life is yours to live

Just because everyone's life is pink
You do not have to paint tours pink too
The Fall as lovely browns
Paint them if it fits you

The Canvas is yours
The colors as well
Create!

The Blame Game

I blame you Portugal!
I blame you for making me leave
when I wanted to stay
for showing me that I wasn't welcome
for showing me that I was just another
number,
and for showing me that humanity
forgot what being Human really means!

I blame you London!
I blame you for making me feel empty,
for showing me the dirt of the human soul,
for showing me the anxiety and stress faces,
and for showing me that humanity
forgot what being Human really means!

I blame you capitalist Society!
I blame you for making a black sheep out of
me,
for showing me that thinking different is
not cool,
for showing me that being myself is morally
wrong,
and for showing me that humanity
forgot what being Human really means!

But above all...
I blame myself!
I blame myself for letting these things put
me down,
for showing them that I was wrong when I
wasn't,
for showing them that I wasn't special when
I am,
and for showing them that I was another one
forgetting about what being human
really means!

It is within You

So,
I forgive you, Portugal
I forgive you, London
I forgive you, capitalist Society
And I must forgive myself too...

Because being human
is loving one another,
is accepting the difference
and unite with each other

So,
I forgive you
And I forgive myself too!

With all my travels
and all my experiences
I came to realize one thing…
We are only miserable because of
ourselves!
Because we choose to…

It's not the social conventions,
It's not the corrupted politics,
It's not the empty meaning religions
It's not the shallow relationships…
It's us!

Always us!
We are the sole root of our own misery,
and shall be no mystery
the antidote for it all

Is, within us!

Until you stop running

from your own **shadow**

You won't be happy!

How old,
How mature,
How woke
were you,
when you met Yourself?

How long,
How deep,
How fully
have you actually met
your real Self?

It is within You

My internal compass
says: "go for it, it's yours to get"

But, my mind, heavily
influenced by the social mindset
tells me to hold on...

In the middle of all of this
my inner Self is always lost!

[remember who you are]

I often feel like this empty canvas
where everyone I cross paths with
leaves a slash of their own paint,
a bit of their own pain
for me to make sense out of it
while I can't even paint
my own canvas myself!

**[You can't love someone right if you
love yourself wrong]**

I Appreciate people
that inhale hate
and exhale Love

We are what we leave behind,
not what we believe we are taking
with us!

[Leave kindness]

When I die
I want people to laugh
Children to play around
Birds singing
Music playing loud!

When I die
I want my ashes
To be spread over the land
So the sea comes
And collects it from the sand

When I die
I only want
To be surrounded by life!

The wind
changes the direction of the waves
and the shape of the sand dunes,
but the sea and the desert
remain the same!

That's the magic of life!

Experiences change our perception
of the world that surround us,
but our core values and ideals
will always remain the same!

[Enjoy the winds that life brings you]

It is within You

I am in a constant flow!
Like a river running to the sea,
but flowing backwards…

Back to the source
Back to the origin,
flowing backwards to my own self!

[find your core and build from within]

As the beautiful flower
Grows in the horrid vase
I grow beautifully
In this social disgrace

[You can too]

It is within You

You can be anything

If You lay in the grass long enough
You will grow roots

If You look into the sky long enough
You will learn how to fly

If You swim in the sea long enough
You will learn how to breathe under
water

You can be anything
And everything is
What You will achieve
If you put your mind into it

Only you know
The whole truth
About your whole being
About your whole life…

Don't let someone else
Tell you otherwise

Never be no one's Luigi
Mário the fuck up of your life!

I am no Marlon Brando
Or Martin Luther King Jr.
But, no one is myself either

And that…

That's fucking awesome!!!

It is within You

I am me, and me is all I can be
If you want to love me,
you'll have to appreciate me
If you won't tolerate the real me
We just can't be...

You see,
I am me,
and me is all I will ever aim to be!

I am not proud my profession

I don't own it
It doesn't own me…
I didn't create it
And it doesn't define me…
It's just what I chose to do!
What I like enough,
to spend hours of my life
doing it,
in order to get paid enough
to actually do what I love!

So no!
I am not proud of my profession

I am proud of my choices!

Nothing in the world is perfect
So why should you?

[Be you, imperfect as you are]

Maybe the grass looks
greener the other side

**Because you don't water
yours for a while**

Make sure you're living
the life you want to tell
your grandchildren about

Ironically

All we have
And all we lack,
Is the exact same thing:

Time!

Make yours count

.

It is within You

When you're a kid
Next week feels like next year…
The wait is unbearable

When you're an adult
Next week feels like yesterday…
If you wait, it is already too late!

Would you change your Life
If you knew you're dying?

Would you maybe…
Tell "that" person that you
love her?

Forgive that friend you
lost contact with?

Travel the world?

Well…

Guess what?
YOU ARE DYING…
Quick as hell!

Most of the times,
We don´t ~~begin~~ again
Because we know
The pain
"the" feeling,
Of all we have been through…

And so,
We don´t ~~begin~~ again
Living the rest of our lives
Just the same
settling out of fear of past pains

Doubt originates Action
which propels Experience
that results
In truly Living

There are only five things
that never stop:

Time
Expansion of universe
Life
Nature
and your Mind

Why do we let all them go
and always try to stop
our minds flow?

Thinking is Evolving
Evolving is Living
and Living is everything

My father always told me:

"You set the limits of your own freedom"

And boy...
it hurt when I realised that
I had been caging myself the whole time

Don't let the last numbers
of your credit card,
a 3 digit code,
control your mind set
or your goals

I feel like a Neanderthal

When,
I hear you talking about social strata
country borders
money rates
and racial profiling,
as if any of that really matters....

I feel like a Neanderthal

When,
I see you working from dawn to dusk
living in a small screen
subjugating your nature to capitalism
and ask to be enslaved by the media,
as if any of that really matters...

I cannot help to feel like a Neanderthal

Someone gladly ~~ignorant~~
someone happy to feel "small"
someone connected to the roots of it
all...

It is within You

We all love to converse
We all love to argue
Suggest, opine, discuss
We all love to post,
Like, follow, and comment…
So much communication choices
And still,
We forget to use our own voices!!

Soul Charmer

What makes you a good person?

Your beautiful words?

Your amazing actions?

Your looks?

I think it's only your instinct

Your true animal side

Nothing more honest that that…

Cuz animal honesty holds no human pride

Be In-sane

We live with a rope
knotted between our dicks
and a shotgun.
If erect
it goes bam!!!

That's how society
controls us,
repressing our instincts
with manipulated ~~rationality~~
based on fear,
caging our soul animal
till insanity…

Someway, somehow
everyone is struggling...

just be kind enough
to understand that

Asking someone to never
make a mistake again
is the same as telling them
to restrain from being human

Allow others to fail
and be ok with that
allow yourself to err
and also be ok with that

Just imagine the Present
as this infinite line...
A line that separates the Past
from the Future
A line so thin
you can't ever step on it

A line that is no more and no less
than a barrier between what you did
and what you will do
being it right or wrong.

What you see, hear, feel right now
is already in the Past…
What you intend to do is yet to come
and is a dream that won't last…
It will come and immediately
cross the line into the histories everlast
It will never linger in the Present
and that's the secret of the human essence…

Life is this constant limbo
of not living the Present
by constantly shifting between what has been
and what is there yet to be
because there's simply no Present to live in

   It's just a line you can't even step on!

It is within You

You either
have something
or you don't...

Unless that something is time
You actually
kind of have and don't have
Time at the same time!

The art of overthinking is the art of
using your own mind to confuse itself!

The liberation of the over thinker
happens upon the realisation
that thoughts must flow naturally
and that any attempt to organise
or even release them using one's mind
is the equivalent as caging a bird
and make it fly for 10 miles
inside the cage, round and round!

Acknowledge the thoughts
and set them free
Allow your mind to think
as if in a river that flows,
fluid, unidirectional…
Don't build a dam where thoughts will
stagnate and become a messy swamp!

Don't dwell over anything
Don't waste your time, your life

Life is a flash
A blink of an eye

It's all it takes,
a simple blink of an eye

Living today,
thinking about tomorrow,
will make you remember today,
as another day of sorrow

Live slow,
don't live to fast...
issues will show,
but surely won't last

Overthinking is a jail
stopping you to prevail
Won't let you enjoy,
will make you fail...
Free yourself, and sail

One moment,
one second,
one decision
It doesn't take much...
Just vision

Point the gun,
press the clutch,
aim for the sun,
feel the trust

You command your own destiny,
not your friends or family
Do whatever you feel,
don't even listen to me

Today is your ~~last~~ day
You press the play...
As hard as it can be,
no matter what others say,
never be afraid
to be whoever you want to be

Live each moment as the last...
Your life is **Yours**!
Have a blast,
they closed the doors...
But you already passed

Sometimes you just fuck it up,
and that's part of life

Who gives a fuck?
Be who you are,
     and Never give up!

What you don't realise yet, is
that while struggling,
the tiniest step
taken in the right direction
will become, one day,
"The" most important one
You have ever walked
towards a whole new You

Changed so much in 12 months
That I can actually say
I was born last year…

We don't need to change the world
but the ~~humanity~~ in it

Be true to your gut

Faking a smile
Is faking an emotion
And faking an emotion
Is cheating on your feelings

Hei…

You look like someone who needs
A tiny word of appreciation…

You are enough!

You are worthy!

You are amazing!

Have a good day stranger

I didn't just do 30 trips around the sun
To settle for anything else but
Greatness!

I.

am.

going.

to.

fucking.

make.

it.

and you will too

I am that kind of guy
that likes to hear a "No"
just to be able to prove
them wrong

The only two things we own
are a powerful mind
and a useful voice

Ironically,
the only two things we settle for
are to be barcoded
and not have a choice

I will never ask you
to think like I do,
only to **think** too!

It's not age nor time that
gives You life experience

It's experience,
that gives you experience

[seek discomfort]

Your worst mistake:

"Just waiting
for the stars
to align
in my favor again"

A good liar becomes so good at lying
That the person he lies the most
is Himself

- tell yourself the truth

It is within You

They bubble wrapped me
They just wanted me to be free
and I never truly faced the world
I almost lost my soul

They loved me more than anything
They protected me from everything
I lived with my eyes closed
I could only see my own nose

I was wearing a sugarcoated coat
cuz I never been an escape goat
Shocked with the brutal world
I almost lost my soul

They raised me to the pedestal
Involuntarily made me feel pivotal
I could not hear the truth
I lived deaf, my whole youth

They cotton candied my bad behaviors
They were always there to cover up
my failures
I stumbled upon the ruthless world
I almost lost my soul 1

They loved me to madness
and for that I will always love
them, regardless
But I almost lost my soul
Gladly, woke up before leaving this
world

Thank you for loving me
Thank you for letting me go
and setting me free
You will always have my love
but while I live
my Soul will belong only to me

I almost lost my soul
You will always have my love
but never my whole inner world
that's up to me to control ₂

Never let your desires
overstep your deepest needs

You deserve all
You have been dreaming about

Don't let anything or anyone
take that away from You

Not even you...

Never turn your back
to adversity
that's how **it** wins

Never resume your Today to:

Finish yesterday's work
or prepare tomorrow's stuff

Never undervalue what you have
Your reality, as bad as it
might seem,
Is someone else's most
treasured dream!

Success

It's not about the social recognition
It's about never being satisfied

It's not about the riches it brings you
It's all about the hard work you do

It's not about being the best of them all
It's about competing against your own
self above all

It's not about an one-time opportunity
It's about enhancing yourself,
relentlessly

Some beg for some change
Some dream of change
Some fight for the change
And then, there's the ones
Who are the ~~Change~~

T.R.Y.

Take. the **R**isk. of being **Y**ou.

Put yourself out there
Show yourself you can do it
Prove yourself you have it
Challenge yourself to fee it

TRY

Seek Discomfort

Comfort is a motherfucker
Comfort is a soul sucker
Comfort is a creativity crusher
Comfort is a mind murderer
Comfort is a motherfucker!

Seek discomfort
Seek inspiration
Seek freedom
Seek love and unity
Seek discomfort,
and you'll find…

You!

I do not have a clue
about what it is
that you hold within You

But I know someone who does
You!

Whatever it is,
put it out there
share it, own it,
love it, live it

Sing about it
Paint it somewhere
Write about it
Perform it somewhere
Express it

*It is within **You** somewhere*

Self Love

Like Ember
it burns inside of You
against the ashes
Waiting for the spreading wind
to break the shackles

Like ember
waiting for the perfect
conditions
to ignite again
to make You whole again

Just like ember
You just need to find it
within

Be the almighty
owner of your
power of will

You and only You can change it!

[Your situation]

The quicker you realize that

"Your freedoms bother a lot of people, and there's absolutely nothing you can do about it"

The quicker you will be happier

You will always be the villain
in someone's heart…

But who cares?

You only need to be the Hero
on your own life and soul!!

— do You

In a world so
desperate to connect,
nobody is connected
with their inner -self

It is within You

Nobody knows more about
yourself
than your own inner light…
It knows you from inside out

It is you!
The one to trust
The one to follow

Do what You love to do
Not what others tell You to

It is within You

As the clouds
gracefully change their shapes
during windy days

Life brings us
our unknown fates
and our unexpected experiences
in all different ways…

If we observe the clouds
and imagine all types
of signs and forms,
why can't we day dream or lives
and stop following the windy storms?

Just think…

In Your life, somethings
will only happen once
and you will never know
which ones are it…

So face every situation
as if it was the first and
last,
being it good or bad

Seize the day

Sometimes we say goodbye
to someone we Love
for the last time
without knowing it is the last time…
And to be honest,
tt works the same way
with our lives
We never know when's our last sigh!

We all have our "Dream life"

- Mine is just to live it!

In my rocking chair with my whiskey in one hand and my weed on the other, while looking at the lake that bathes my wooden cabin in the middle of the Canadian Rockies, I grabbed my phone and changed my online status to:

"I'm extremely busy"

Try to be a cat
in a world of Pavlov's dogs…
a world of "who's a good boy?"
All behaving accordingly
just waiting for the rewards,
not being themselves
all played as toys

You all follow trends
just to be fashionable…

However

You forget that you get so ordinary
that nobody else notices you!

You are just another
like any other!

We are just another
drop of water
in this time vortex
through space

So,
Own it
Make it count

As one last drop
can make the glass full…

We are just one drop
but we all count!!!

We are nothing less
than dust
blown by the winds
of time

Time is so unfair
Time is so fucking unfair
I would even say discriminatory
Time is the most motherfucker
of all motherfuckers!
I hate Time in its most inner core
I hate Time's foundation,
even dare to say, it's creation
that might extend my hate to its
creators

I mean,
Yesterday was time to pack to travel
Today, a week after, is time to unpack
and it passed like only an hour
Time is so fucked up,
sometimes 3 hours take 3 days
and 3 days take a minute

Time is so unfair
Time is so fucking unfair,
so unfair, and so random
that you probably didn't even notice it,
but from the first line to this same one
I got older, you got older
and some others are gone and over!!

I fucking hate Time
and our inability to control it
Or to be fully honest,
our inability to truly enjoy it

It is within You

Every single moment, every single second of our lives is being recorded in our brains as an infinite VHS cassette…

If we could access greater parts of our brains we would, not only be able to review those same moments, as would be able to relive them with all the feelings, emotions, and senses we felt in the first place. But, as we can only access around 10% of our brains capabilities, we can only remember certain aspects of our existence, and often can't even select what we remember or not.
We still have all that infinite information taped and stored on our natural computer, but we often only get memories about special moments or random situations that a smell or a song brought us back to!

Exactly as a shelf full of old VHS tapes. We always have the wedding one, our mums 50th birthday, and our daughter's graduation…
And then you have several others that you never remember you stored, but they are there, and when an old friend shows up, you remember it and go pick it up…

Every single second counts, every single action, every single word, every single interaction!

Remember that everyday…
It's a tape recording from birth to death!

The most altruistic act
is to plant a tree
knowing you will never enjoy
it's shade or it's fruits

The most altruist act
is to do something good
for your peers
knowing they will never be able
to return the favours

It is within You

Cold makes us contract all muscles
Putting together all our molecules
With the sole purpose of warming up
our bodies

Humanity should act the same way
Embracing each one of us together
Using Love as the warming agent
Leaving out no one
Touching everybody the same

What moves the World
Is not money or fame…
It's Love!

And how you share that Love
is the true key to win the game

Just add
Don't take

Add smiles to the table
Add positivity to conversations
Add meaningful words
Add helpful actions
Add compliments to the weak
Add joyfulness while walking
the street

Just add
Don't take

The world is already too dark
Already too mad
Already in lack
Of positivity and equity...

So don't take
Just add...

You can and should
care about others,
but ultimately you
must care first about

Yourself!!!

It is within You

I realised I have been running from my life
Living in the past like it is mine
Embracing the darkness where the sun doesn't shine
I realised I lost myself,
and live out of sight
Living in boring grey when I could live in stunning red bright

I realised my Present is guided by my past drive
Where I had someone by my side
Someone that is no longer for me to call mine
And that's how I have been wasting my life

Running from it like running from fire
An invisible one that doesn't actually burn anything but my mind!
I realised that moving on is fine
Not running but facing the fear in the eye
Embrace the pain and own it as mine

I realised that running from my life is just a sign
A sign telling me that I keep running but not moving
A sign that I keep hurting but not healing
A sign that I am running with my feet but I am stuck in my mind!

I realised I need to stop running
Start facing
Maybe do some closing
And then be free for the actual Living!!

Hear this:

Sound is something material because sound is no less than waves moving graciously in specific rhythms and frequencies through thin air. And this waves create a harmonious turmoil that actually change their surroundings. So, we can all agree that sound is material and not some esoteric concept.

Now ruminate on this:

If you dream of something you really like or want, that's nothing else than a dream in your head, an idea, something not tangible at all, something you cannot grasp and hold in your hand.
However, if you verbalize that idea, it becomes material, just because sound, as we established before, is indeed a physical entity…

So, yes… dream as much as you want, and say you dreams out loud as much as you can! They might not become true straight away but its physical form is now out there because you made the shift from abstract to objective, from concept to concrete.
That's the first step to dream materialization, the transformation of an intangible idea from the immaterial world into existence, into reality.

Speak your truth and materialize your dreams!

There's a big difference between
wanting and needing something…

You might want to eat chocolates
everyday
Maybe one or two,
but you don't need diabetes do you?

[want what you need, not what you want]

The more material you have
The less spiritual you live
The more you clock the time
The lesser of life you live

It is within You

We all **fight** for better jobs,
fancier cars and houses
We all **long** for the ultimate gadget,
shinier clothes, and even shinier spouses
We all **search** for the 'gram sweet honey
for easy fame and that extra money
We all do it for the wealth and material
well-being
but when someone asks us:
What do you want to
leave behind as your legacy?
What do you want other people
to say about you when you leave this
world?
When someone asks us:
What do you want your grandkids
to be proud of about you?
What do you want
to think about on your last breath
when you disconnect one last time?
We will say something not even remotely
related
to all the **search**, **fight** and **longing**
we so passionately did our entire lives...
And that must suck, no?
Driving all the way north
when we wanted to go south...
Just because our GPS was upside down
just because our faulty internal compass
put us out of route.
Realising that, at the end of the road?
That must suck, no?
Realign your priorities, not when you
depart
not when you are arriving
but all the time… during the whole trip!

Sunset

I hope you really appreciate
The whole idea of it…
Waiting 30 minutes to an hour,
For a few seconds of pure bliss

Just like anything else in our lives
The journey is always
where the magic lies!

We want to run before walking
We want to be adults before ripening
We want to fuck before connecting
We want to excel before learning
We want to arrive before departing
We want to eat before cooking
We want to party before working
We want to be successful before
hustling
We want to be pleased before
pleasing
We want to be the best before
practicing
We want to be loved before loving
We want to be accepted by hating
We want loyalty without committing
We want the trophy without even
playing

We want everything besides what we
need
We want it all, and we forget to
live!

We want to live but we are dying
We are not the Human race but humans
racing...

[The journey is worth living]

Why would You want to know Your own
future?
Once You know it, You owe to it
And then there's nothing else worthy to
live for!

Imagine knowing the end of a movie
when you are in the middle of watching
it…
Two things will happen:

1. You skip to another movie as that
   one is no longer challenging
2. You watch the whole thing waiting
   for the announced end without even
   noticing the whole plot, missing
   the whole point of the story
   itself

So,
why would You want to know Your own
future?

**Don't try to miss the whole point of
life, just Live it**

We are never truly in control of anything. We might feel a stronger sense of control in some specific situations accordingly to our surroundings and expectations, but anything can still happen at any given time or place.
And "that" everything will always be out of our control.

Let it go

Outgrown

Sometimes you just outgrow
and that leaves you alone

You just outgrow jobs, people,
friends
and that leaves you alone

You just outgrow relationships,
places, trends
and that leaves you alone

Sometimes you just outgrow
and being alone is the first step
to higher grounds, a higher you

And all the rest has to stay behind,
just below, because sometimes…

You just outgrow!

"Let him hit his head on the wall
until he learns that it hurts"

He hit his head against the wall
so many times,
so many nights,
till eventually
He ~~woke~~ ~~up~~ and smiled...

Knowing that we would not fear the
night
Not that day
Not today
Not ever again!

It is within You

Pain is like the sea wave ripples
after a boat passes by
Hits you, less and less,
every day,
less and less,
and eventually it's gone…
And there's no more mess
just a fearless fire
a light from within
that moves you on

The comfort zone
Won't allow you to move on
You are a human being
Always changing,
Always growing,
Always different,
But always the same!
Always coherent,
No matter what You've
became…
Embrace the change
Embrace your own way

When you are conscious of your own feet
it's because you're not comfortable
in your shoes and how they fit…

Likewise,
when you are comfortable with your life,
you are not truly conscious of it!

    — **Numb to reality, in the zone of
      comfortability**

You never know what is on the
other side of the wall
Until you open "that" door...

Insist,
Practice,
Persist,
Don't quit...

You got this!!!

Smiling is a habit, Practice it!

Being Yourself is a habit,
        Own it!

It is within You

What others see, doesn't define me

A philosophical essay
by Soul Charmer

"Ego is a social institution with no
physical reality. The ego is simply
your symbol of yourself"

— Alan Watts

We are what we delimit ourselves to be, in relation to the world around us and the interactions we have with it on a daily basis.

In addition, we are to others what they want/need us to be, and that does not define whom, indeed, we turn out to be. Everyone sees you accordingly to their own past experiences and associations with their own ideals and knowledge, as limited/open as they might be.

Fighting to fit in, is a lost war against the world and ultimately against ourselves. As much as we want to fit in, we will never be able to know exactly what others expect from us, we can adapt as much as we need, but we will never be truly what others seem to see on us. There is this eternal paradox, where we fight to be what others expect us to be, to look, to feel, to do, as we think they would like us to. But, since we are not able to step into their shoes, or think their thoughts or look through their eyes, we will never be able to sense what they sense of us. And, if we do not grasp this fundamental principle, how come can we actually please them?

What I am is that and only that…
I am what I came to be, and I will
never be able to show my inwards to
anyone else, ever, which itself turns
into an invisible barrier that we were
given at birth and that will endure
till we die. I'll never be able to
make anyone feel what I feel, see what
I see, and sense what I sense, and
that will always create a void between
what I really am, and what I appear
to be in the eyes of my peers.

Let me exemplify with a lucid dream I
had:

I live in a two bedroom flat in London, where my friends use to come for dinner and some drinks. One night, in bed, while waiting for my brain to shut down, I started imagining that I was in the mind of one of my friends that frequently come to my place. I could feel his feelings and see all he was seeing as he approached my door and rang the bell. All was clear to me as I was actually him. I climbed the staircase and the door was already open. I went in and took my shoes of in the entrance hall while looking at all the Lego sets that myself (the dreamer) have in my own flat. As myself approaches my friend (which I am controlling), I can recognize my own body, my own form, own clothes and mannerisms... I recognize the walk and the smell but for some reason I cannot see my own face or recognize my own voice. The morning after, I woke up with this idea in my head again, and managed to imagine being in a different friends mind, seeing me in a more intimate situation as I was in the shower. In her mind I could recognize again the body of myself and the moles I have and the gestures I routinely make while bathing myself, but again I could not see at any point my own face or hear my own voice.

This experience shed some light in my head. I can't see my face in these lucid dreams, or even listen to my voice because those are egoistic constructs of who I believe to be. We all hear our voices differently when we recorded it, and we all think its rubbish right? That is because we hear our own voice differently than anyone else does. We hear our voice and it sounds melodic and perfect for the bag of skin we are contained in, but when we exteriorize it, put it out of our being, by recording it, it feels like it doesn't belong to us anymore and it feels weird to listen to it. At this point, we have no idea what others think of our voice and how good or bad it sounds to them, but since it sounds so good to us when within us, we believe our voice is actually perfect and fits flawlessly on our being… This is the unrealistic symbol of ourselves that Alan Watts talks about. "One must hear my voice and hear how beautiful or perfect of a match it is to my body and personality"- that's what our ego tells us, and we go on believing it. However, the ones surrounding us have different sound receptors and even if the sound waves are the same, their amplifiers and modulators are different, hence, why some people love Opera and for others, listening to it is the most dreadful experience they have ever had to endure.

Same phenomenon happens with our faces and the way we see ourselves. The only moment I see myself is when I look into a mirror, and even then, I am not truly seeing myself as I "see" myself inside of my head, as a mirror is a reflection that can be manipulated, and not truly represent the actual reality of the being. I "see" my face in my own head and I know all my features and starts and ends but I can't see into my own head, the eye balls down rotate 360 degrees and what I see in the mirror is what I believe I am and that image quite often differs from what my ego tells me. Let's put it this way: we all have days where we get up of the bed and feel beautiful for no apparent reason, even before looking in the mirror, but when we do look into the mirror, this feeling of grace gets extrapolated and we could not agree more with ourselves and say it out loud "I look awesome today"! We all have been there right?

This is our ego talking, our own image of ourselves that manipulates what we see in the mirror and makes us feel even better about ourselves – this is the fit in feeling.

The reason I could not see my face in my own lucid dream, when embodying another person, is that of that I never truly saw my own face! I know my face within my mind, I recognize it, I feel it and can sense its features, but I never really saw it if not through a mirror. That mirror is my friends mind when looking at myself…

Everyone around us will see our face and hear our voice differently, and there is no way, at least an attainable one for now, for us with the existing technology, to understand, see, feel or sense what anyone of those people have on their minds about us and how we present ourselves to them. We are what our Ego tells us to be and as much as we try to adapt to fit in, we will only fit in if the surroundings are willing to accommodate us!

If we don't really know what others truly see on us or feel about us, we will never be able to adapt in order to fit it. One can argue that we can ask what they see or feel about us, but once again that will be a misleading manifestation of their own Ego based on their own experiences and constructed conventions and not the true manifestation of our own bodies, souls and minds.

Just try this small exercise:

Ask your Mum how she hears your voice, how she sees your face, how she feels about your presence, and then ask the stranger that sells you bread in your hometown bakery and who you never say a kind word to, the exact same questions! The answers will be so different that you will feel like a completely different person, and still know whom you really are and try to compare it against their answers. That's when your Ego comes into play. It will tell you to choose the most pleasant answers, the ones that make you feel good about yourself, and correlate them with the image you have built about who you are. This allows you to fit in where you feel you are most accepted, or on the other hand making you try to adapt to be more likeable to the bakery employee and as consequence, more settle in his environment.

This is the root of our irritations/frustrations when someone tells us some heartfelt truths about our behavior that we relentlessly want to fight back as we built the idea of "I" based on our own beliefs and experiences which will always differ from anyone else's that is not in your head. However, the need to belong is so strong that we endure this emotional pain in order to praise our Egos by managing to change a stranger's perception of who we are in order to be accepted in their environment as equals. Basically, we lie to ourselves to please someone who we owe nothing, in order to please this non-physical reality that only lives in our heads, and is the product of the social conventions we were raise upon.

"**We buy things we don't need with money we don't have to impress people we don't like**"
       - Dave Ramsey

So, our ideal of -self is an image upon construct that was fed to us since birth until the day we call present. The bed you laid in, the toys you had the privilege to toy with, the school your parents afforded, or not, to send you to, the friends you made, the currency you used, the food you ate, the TV shows you watched, the books you read, the games you played, the teachings you were taught, all shaped who you are today, all made you believe you are who you believe you are. After all, at birth and continuously during our lives, we are this kind of empty bottle where day-by-day, we place another grain of sand in a specific location (read personality traits/experiences/learnings in an empty canvas called mind) and build an image. Kind of a landscape within that bottle - your ego - your image of your own -self seen by yourself, felt by your own senses, thought by your own thoughts, given to you by your own choices and your own actions upon the possibilities provided to you in the environment you were lucky (or not) to be born and raised in.

All seems to fit in perfectly just like in this sand art bottle, where each and every single grain of sand is as important as the rest to conceive the final grand piece. Each grain is an experience you have lived, a skill you have learnt, a sound listened, a feeling felt, a bit of your own existence that was given to you by any external stimulae.

What everyone sees of you is the perfect and complete image that you are now, the boat floating in the ocean water or the sunset on the beach that your bottle of sand strongly and proudly shows off to him or her, with all this textures and intricate designs – the "whole picture" per se. You show yourself daily as this awesome and beautifully put collection of attributes that everyone can admire and congratulate you about, and the longer this goes on, the better and prettier you feel. You start to take pride on yourself as this amazing bottle everyone wants to grasp and behold, you get more and more recognition and adoration and that makes our sand shine even in the shadows of our own most deadly fear – rejection. This is our ego trying to fit in where there is not space to be in the first place as we do not even know where that place is or, ultimately what it is like at all.

Just contemplate this second exercise:

Hold on to a sand art bottle and admire it for a few seconds. There's this astounding beauty in it right? Different colors arranged in this perfect sequence bringing life to an absolute marvelous image of some kind of nature landscape or an animal. You hold it, turn it, play around with it, and all you can see is the landscape and the amazing piece of art that bottle is. The bottle is, at your eyes, a solo object as the sand is now contained within it, and you can't get hold of it, and you either like that object for what it represents to you, or you don't! You know what it is, you know how it was grossly made, but you don't know the meticulous process of making it as everyone does it differently.

Now, open that bottle, and spread all the sand grains on the table before you, and simply contemplate... What do you see? Is it the same object now? Is it still beautiful to you, does it represent the same as it did before?

I am sure the answers to those questions are starting to haunt you. There is no more sunset landscape view or vivid colors arranged in a symmetrical or melodically way... All you see now is the raw content of the meticulous process of making such art piece, and honestly, you do not understand it at all right?
Even if different, you are still holding the same object but without the magic of "the process" of actually making it. You have the contents and the recipient, but you do not know the detailed process to assemble it together again.

This is what we are. We are the meticulous process of making our own selves, and not the product that everyone sees... Everyone can perceive the art piece as a whole, with their own biased interpretations, and love it or loathe it, but only you know the process behind your own construction, behind your own existence and your own beauty.

And as much as you choose the sand grains you built yourself with, you will never be able to show the external observers, the process of making your own art becoming real, as that is intrinsic to you and only you. And so, you will be led to believe that when people adore your final state – your full bottle – that you are what they see, and when they don't like it, you will try to rearrange your sand grains to produce a new landscape that suits their tastes, that **FITS** their measurements, but you will never change your contents – experiences that shaped you – hence why what they see will never define what and who you are.

This is the root of the old saying "People can't change". I truly believe that people can adapt and morph accordingly to the need, but in their deep core, we are the meticulous process that made us, and unfortunately (or not) there's no time machine to change that process, and so forth, people can't actually change…

So,
What I am, is not what you
see/feel/sense about me… I am one
within myself, and a million others
for you to see.

What others see,
doesn't define me

Chameleon

Each and every one of you
that met me once or more
in your life

Each one of you, knows one of me
I am no same personal entity
for more than one of you

I am whole when I meet myself
but apart from that
I am a multimillion personality
according to the multimillion
different people that meet me

It is within You

It is

within You

It is within You

Printed in Poland
by Amazon Fulfillment
Poland Sp. z o.o., Wrocław

56627366R00101